Edward Hetherington is a practising barrister and a member of Albion Chambers in Bristol. He is instructed by the prosecution and defence in complex and serious cases across England and Wales. He is a Grade 4 CPS Panel Advocate and a member of the Regulatory Advocates in Health & Safety and Environmental Law Panel. Before coming to the Bar, Edd was a university law lecturer. He remains involved in designing and delivering bespoke lectures to groups of legal professionals and organisations. He is regularly involved in advocacy training as well as providing accredited CPD and training to professionals from across the country.

Edward obtained a law degree from the University of Durham, before going on to gain a Master's Degree. He was Called to the Bar (Middle Temple) in 2006, having been awarded the JJ Powell scholarship.

Covid-19 and Health and Safety Law – The Essential Guide

Covid-19 and Health and Safety Law – The Essential Guide

Edward Hetherington
Barrister, Middle Temple
LLB (Hons) (Dunelm) LLM

Law Brief Publishing

Published 2021 by Law Brief Publishing, an imprint of Law Brief Publishing Ltd
30 The Parks
Minehead
Somerset
TA24 8BT

www.lawbriefpublishing.com

Paperback: 978-1-913715-90-8

To Mam and Dad.

PREFACE

"Some lawyers are born into H&S specialism. Other lawyers seek out H&S specialism. The rest just happen to be in the Clerks' Room at the worst possible moment."

Health and Safety law has evolved enormously in a very short amount of time. From the first tentative common law duties imposed upon 'masters' in an attempt to ensure that their 'servants' were not merely used until damaged and then discarded, up to the modern era of protective measures for all at work, the landscape has become unrecognisable.

The 21st century risk-averse culture, labelled 'Health and Safety gone mad' by those who presumably pine for the good old days of unguarded blades and minors as miners, had settled into a landscape of close regulation, enforced in the UK by the Health and Safety Executive and an increasingly robust justice system.

At least, that is, until 2020. The global coronavirus pandemic has changed the way we all work. Lockdowns, working from home, social distancing and face masks were unthinkable before March of last year, whereupon they became the norm for all of us overnight.

The purpose of this book is to identify some of the areas of health and safety law where the virus and its consequences will have the most immediate impact and to provide practical guidance on meeting those challenges and how the law is likely to respond. I hope it is a useful text and contributes to the general dialogue of how workplaces can cope in the short term and evolve thereafter.

My thanks to all who have supported my career in the law, to my colleagues at Albion Chambers and to the excellent clerking and support staff who have kept us running through the most trying of times. My family and friends deserve the deepest gratitude of all, for tolerating my peculiarities on an entirely voluntary basis.

I am grateful to all at Law Brief Publishing for first allowing me to write this and then for their advice and assistance.

Any errors in this work are mine. The legal position is described as of 1st February 2021.

Edward Hetherington
February 2021

CONTENTS

CHAPTER ONE

COVID-19 AND RISK ASSESSMENTS

Risk assessments are now well-established as a key obligation of responsible employers. All employers have a specific legal duty to assess the risks to the health and safety of employees (and risks to the health and safety of persons not in their employment) to which they are exposed while they are at work.

The underlying statement of an employer's obligation within the Health and Safety at Work etc Act 1974 is that "*[i]t shall be the duty of every employer to ensure, so far as is reasonably practicable, the health, safety and welfare at work of all his employees.*"[1]

Taking the time to produce a thorough and practical assessment of the hazards involved in each aspect of the workforce's operation, plus devising and implementing a coherent and protective series of measures to manage or remove such hazards, is the first step in ensuring compliance with that key obligation within health and safety law[2].

The statutory instrument which specifically make risk assessments a legal requirement is the Management of Health and Safety at Work

---

[1] section 2(1) *Health and Safety at Work etc. Act 1974*

[2] In *R v Chargot Ltd* [2008] UKHL 73, it was emphasised that the aim of the health and safety legislation in the UK is to achieve a result, not to prescribe the method by which that result is received.

Regulations (MHSWR) 1999. Regulation 3 provides (so far as is relevant) that:

> *"(1) Every employer shall make a suitable and sufficient assessment of—*
>
> > *(a) the risks to the health and safety of his employees to which they are exposed whilst they are at work; and*
> >
> > *(b) the risks to the health and safety of persons not in his employment arising out of or in connection with the conduct by him of his undertaking,*
>
> *for the purpose of identifying the measures he needs to take to comply with the requirements and prohibitions imposed upon him by or under the relevant statutory provisions…"*

There is very little guidance in caselaw[3] as to how risk assessments should be written, but there is an Approved Code of Practice which accompanies the 1999 Regulations. By virtue of s17 of the HSWA 1974 that Code of Practice is admissible in criminal proceedings and failure to comply is prima facie evidence of breach of duty.

If a business is visited by HSE inspectors, either during a spot-check or following an incident on their premises which attracts the attention of the inspectors, is it highly likely that one of their first requests will be to see the risk assessment files held by the company. The ability to comply, and the quality of the documentation therein, is likely to set the tone for the subsequent interactions between the parties.

[3] A rare example might be *Bailey v Command Security Services* [2001] All ER 352 (QBD) on the rather limited area of sending security guards to patrol other companies' premises.

When drafting a risk assessment, an employer is well-advised to consult employees, union reps[4] and (if applicable) their occupational health or health and safety representatives. Employees are far more likely to appreciate why procedures are in place and to follow them if they have been given a voice in developing those health and safety practices in the work environment.

However, that is not to say that formal and costly consultation is required before every risk assessment is concluded. Some consultations are specific to one particular role or task and it would be impractical to expect employers to gain staff approval for every minor policy which is devised. It is sufficient that consultation should form part of the general risk assessment process. In practice, most employers conduct a general assessment to identify the key risks and control measures, and then a second brief assessment of the risks by the employees about to embark on the job.

So what difference does the COVID pandemic make to this settled legal position? First, any business needs to start by updating their risk assessment to manage the risk of coronavirus in their business. This will help employees and others to understand what they should do to work safely and protect other people who visit work premises.

This update can either be done by expanding and amending an existing risk assessment, or by creating an entirely new addendum or distinct risk assessment to cover the particular perils associated with the pandemic and the steps to be taken to manage them.

If you have fewer than five employees, you don't have to write anything down, but it might help if you do. A risk assessment is not merely a theoretical exercise, it must be possible to demonstrate that

---

[4] See *EC v UK* [1994] ICR 664 and the Health and Safety (Consultation with Employees) Regulations 1996.

it has taken place and a documentary record is the easiest way to achieve this.

As an employer, there is a legal duty to protect people from harm. This includes taking reasonable steps to protect workers and others from coronavirus. What constitutes "reasonable steps" will vary from business to business, but against a backdrop of unprecedent public health measures such as the national lockdowns imposed by the government, it is clear that a significant level of assessment and action is required by most businesses.

Within a risk assessment an employer should look at what work activity or situations might cause transmission of the virus, who could be at risk, how likely it is that someone could be exposed and then act to remove the activity or situation, or if this isn't possible, to control the risk.

A Public Health England report entitled '*COVID-19: Review of Disparities in Risks and Outcomes*'[5] has shown initial evidence to suggest that some groups of people may be at more risk of being infected and/or an adverse outcome if infected. Groups at particular risk appear to be those from Black and Minority Ethnic (BAME) backgrounds, older people and those living in disadvantaged areas. Employers should consider this in a risk assessment, although it will obviously be the case that some of those groups are easier to protect through workplace measures than others.

Practical measures can include putting in place social distancing measures, staggering shifts and providing additional handwashing facilities. Moving those employees in "at risk" groups away from customer-facing roles will be one potential way of reducing risk, but

[5] Published at https://www.gov.uk/government/publications/covid-19-review-of-disparities-in-risks-and-outcomes, dated 2 June 2020.

equally steps such as the provision of appropriate PPE might be sufficient to prevent taking such a drastic step. Whatever steps are taken, they should match the measures which have been identified and justified in the risk assessment.

CHAPTER TWO

PPE AND CORONAVIRUS

The coronavirus pandemic has not changed the underlying duty of an employer to protect people in the workplace from health and safety risks. This includes making sure they are not exposed to hazardous substances as part of their work. Employers therefore have duties concerning the provision and use of personal protective equipment (PPE) at work.

Personal protective equipment (PPE) protects the user against health or safety risks at work. It includes different types of respiratory protective equipment (RPE), such as oral/nasal respirators. It can also include items such as safety helmets, gloves, eye protection, high-visibility clothing, safety footwear and safety harnesses.

Face coverings, of the kind which are encouraged by the government as a measure to reduce disease transmission, are not in fact PPE. This is because they are not designed to protect wearers from work-related hazardous substances and in practice they do not so protect. They may protect others, but not the wearer, against the spread of coronavirus.

The use of face coverings as a public health protection measure during the coronavirus pandemic in England falls under the Health Protection (Coronavirus, Wearing of Face Coverings in a Relevant Place) (England) Regulations 2020. Separate regulations and guidance apply for public use of face coverings in Scotland and in Wales.

These Regulations place the obligation firmly on individuals to ensure that they wear a face covering when in public places.

Enforcement is by police involvement and prosecution, so it does not place particular legal burdens on employers or occupiers of premises,

PPE for protection against coronavirus is generally only required for certain healthcare activities. In a non-clinical setting, there is no need to provide different PPE than you would normally have provided before the pandemic started.

Selection and Use of PPE

The approach of the HSE, in explaining and advising on how to interpret the relevant legislation, is that PPE should be a last resort, used only when all other control measures have failed to manage a risk satisfactorily[6]. In deciding whether PPE is required, employers must consider who is exposed and to what harmful substance, duration and extent of the exposure and the need for the exposure.

Once a need for PPE is identified, employers should choose and source products which are CE marked in accordance with the Personal Protective Equipment (Enforcement) Regulations 2018. Consideration must be given to the selection of equipment which is well suited to the actual user(s), bearing in mind the size, fit and weight of the PPE.

If the users are permitted to be involved in the process of selecting their own PPE, then experience suggests that they will be more likely to use it.

---

[6] However, once PPE is necessary to address a risk which cannot be controlled by other means, the courts have historically interpreted the duty to provide appropriate PPE as an absolute one. See *North Somerset Council v Farmiloe* [2004] PIQR 22.

The current legislation which refers to the supply of personal protective equipment is the Personal Protective Equipment Regulation 2016/425, which is enforced by the Personal Protective Equipment (Enforcement) Regulations 2018. HSE are the enforcing authority for the supply of PPE that is designed for use at work.

If more than one item of PPE is worn at the same time, it is necessary to make sure that they are mutually compatible. Goggles can interfere with mask seals and so on. If necessary, provide instruction and training to end users including good practice and common risks of misuse.

When training, or devising procedures around the use of PPE, clarity and detail are important. An employer cannot assume that employees will necessarily exercise common sense without being properly trained. Such procedures should avoid ambiguity. Likewise an employer should never allow vague or imprecise exemptions, such as excusing PPE for "quick" tasks. If a task requires PPE then it should always and without exception be undertaken only by those using appropriate equipment in a proper manner.

The proper use of PPE must be monitored and reviewed. Updating the training given on a regular basis is key, so that it reflects the practical reality of usage. It is the responsibility of an employer to replace worn PPE and to check that it is being used properly by undertaking meaningful checks and inspections. Tolerating a culture of lax PPE usage will open up an employer to significant risks in the event of an incident which is investigated by the HSE.

Maintenance of PPE

PPE must be properly looked after and stored when not in use. If it is reusable it must be cleaned and kept in good condition. The duty to maintain is a strict and absolute one, although it applies only to functionality and not irrelevant matters such as cosmetic appearance, per *Fytche v Wincanton Logistics plc*[7].

It is important to consider using the right replacement parts which match the original, taking advice from suppliers where appropriate. Where appropriate replacement PPE is available it must be in good enough condition and maintained as if it were first choice. Employers using PPE should have a clear policy, preferably in writing, specifying who is responsible for maintenance and how it is to be done referring to method and frequency.

Employees must make proper use of PPE and report its loss or destruction or any fault in it. A requirement that they do so should be imposed, enforced and communicated in clear terms when they are trained in use of the equipment.

The IWGB Litigation

In the case of R (IWGB) v Secretary of State for Work and Pensions & Ors[8], judgment was handed down on 13 November 2020. The Independent Workers' Union of Great Britain (IWGB) brought an application for judicial review in the High Court, seeking a declaration that the United Kingdom had failed properly to implement into national

[7](2004) 4 All ER 221

[8] [2020] EWHC 3050 (Admin)

law two EU directives from 1989 relating to the health and safety of those at work.

The union's main point was that that those directives require EU member states to provide protections to 'workers', whereas the implementing UK legislation covers only 'employees'. This disproportionately affects those in the 'gig economy'.

There were two main UK legislative provisions at issue. The first was section 44 of the Employment Rights Act (ERA) 1996 which provides, among other things, that all employees have a right not to be subjected to detriment for leaving or refusing to come to work in circumstances where they have a reasonable belief they are in "serious and imminent danger". The other was Regulation 4 of the PPE at Work Regulations 1992, which requires employers to ensure that suitable PPE is provided to employees who may be exposed to a risk to their health or safety while at work, except where such risk is adequately controlled by other effective means.

The High Court concluded that those provisions failed to implement the respective EU directives correctly by not providing the same level of protection for workers as for employees. It granted the IWGB a declaration to that effect and the Government did not take up its right to seek leave to appeal.

The Health and Safety at Work Act 1974 duties on employers, for the most part, do not extend to workers. That is suddenly a questionable approach, although many employers will have long ago chosen to treat individuals who work alongside each other in the same way, irrespective of their contractual status. However, there may be situations where employers choose to treat workers such as by requiring workers to provide their own PPE or by not providing homeworking risk assessments.

But what about Brexit? The EU Withdrawal Act provides that any UK law passed or made before the end of the transition period must still be interpreted, as far as possible, in accordance with EU law. However, the government is now free to change the law as it sees fit, which is unlikely in the short-term to lead to more good news for 'gig workers'.

CHAPTER THREE

SOCIAL DISTANCING AND THE LAW

Social distancing means keeping people apart to help reduce the spread of infection. Where possible, you should keep people two metres apart. If this is not possible, then a duty-holder must go on to consider possible additional measures to mitigate the consequences of physical proximity.

Within the UK some rules about social distancing may be different in the devolved nations. However, the HSE regulates in each of these countries. You should check the public health guidance for the country you are in to ensure the most recent guidance is implemented. This can be found on the HSE website.

You must ensure that workers and other people visiting your workplace understand and comply with the measures you put in place. This will usually mean in practice that you put signs up to ensure people understand how to move around and negotiate any physical measures which are in place.

Social distancing must form part of a business' COVID-specific risk assessment and is one of the steps designated by the HSE as being essential before any workplace can be considered COVID-secure.

Of course each workplace will be different in terms of how social distancing is approached. The physical makeup of the premises will be a factor to consider, as will the nature of the work and how distancing can be accommodated whilst remaining functional. However, there are a number of universal steps which should at least be considered and it would be wise to include all of them in any written risk assessment, to show that they have been borne In mind, even if your ultimate conclusion is that in your particular workplace they are not practicable.

The first such step is the use of floor tape or paint to mark work areas, impose one-way systems or divide corridors. Where workplaces are in close proximity, reflect upon whether they could be arranged so that employees are working side-by-side rather than face-to-face. Once staff are in place, take any steps which can sensibly limit the movement of people within and between buildings.

Also consider pinch points in your premises such as narrow corridors, staircases, doorways and storage areas. Perhaps they can be made to be one-way or else a "give way" system devised and imposed[9].

Common Areas

Common areas might include break rooms, bathrooms, toilets, canteens, meeting spaces and any other rooms or spaces used by many people. The potential for viral spread is increased in such areas and so effective measures of control must be implemented.

The first step is to identify such common spaces within the premises controlled by your organisation and to review them.

You may need to put in place a combination of control measures to keep people safe. This can include limiting the number of people who enter such spaces, reducing furniture, placing screens between seating

[9] Bearing in mind the obligations under Reg 12 of the Workplace (Health Safety and Welfare) Regulations 1992 to ensure that the floor surfaces in the workplace are kept from being uneven or slippery.

points or marking out areas on the floor which should be avoided. It will rarely be permissible to simply close areas which employees use for rest and breaks[10].

Many employers will need to apply these principles to rest areas or break areas. The pandemic conditions do not remove the obligations upon employers to ensure all workers, including those visiting premises for work, have somewhere to rest and eat and should also provide facilities to heat food or water for hot drinks. Wherever food is being prepared or consumed, good hand hygiene is of course important. In canteens or refectories it is better if food, cutlery and condiments can be brought to diners at their table. Employers can also consider staggering the times at which employees take their meal breaks, open up other spaces for eating

There remains of course a legal duty to provide adequate toilet facilities that are safe to access[11]. These could be staff, visitor or customer facilities. This applies to any workers (including subcontractors, visiting tradesmen and so on), and any visitors or customers, who enter a workplace.

The legal responsibility to promote access to these facilities lies with the controller of the premises. Prohibiting access for any reason, including as an infection control measure, is unlawful. Handwashing is an essential element of the virus control strategy and so it would be wholly inappropriate to simply close such facilities as will be most frequently used for cleansing and where hot running water is readily available.

However, it will often be necessary for some adjustments to be made This may well include taking certain static facilities out of use when

---

10 Reg 25 of the 1992 Regulations.

11 Reg 20 of the Workplace (Health Safety and Welfare) Regulations 1992.

they are less than two metres apart. If this includes toilet facilities such as urinals, the reduction must be balanced against the need to ensure that a premises will still have a sufficient number of toilets for the number of users and visitors.

Where social distancing in toilet facilities becomes impractical, such as where a particular set of toilets is simply too small, then companies may have to put in place systems such as 'one in, one out'.

Accommodation

Employers who provide accommodation for their workers should consider steps which they could implement in order to keep workers safe whilst they are in accommodation and working. These measures should be included in the risk assessment.

Common steps will be to minimise the number of people staying in communal accommodation, keep workers who stay overnight in close proximity together in daytime work tasks, regular health checks and if any worker develops symptoms then their 'bubble' should all self-isolate. Any steps taken to prevent viral exposure must not have a detrimental impact on other areas of safety, especially fire safety.

Arriving and Leaving Work

Safe systems must be devised for the entry and egress of staff and visitors. This may include having separate entrances for staff and customers, for example. Duty-holders must take precautions to limit the chances of anyone with coronavirus entering their premises. This could be by placing signs, or if practicable a member of staff, such as a security officer, asking entrants if they have had recent symptoms or tests.

As well as working from home, staggered start times could help reduce having too many members of staff arrive at once. This may also reduce the burden on public transport if your employees use it to travel to work. Other steps may include using different entrances for those working in different parts of the building.

Companies should provide handwashing facilities at entry and exit points, or hand sanitiser where handwashing is not possible. It will usually be best to avoid using touch-based security devices such as keypads. If they are essential, make sure they are cleaned and disinfected regularly and there is a handwashing or sanitising point immediately after them.

It will always be advisable to put in place procedures for dealing with deliveries, such as a queue system and a hatch or window for accepting them. Handwashing facilities should be provided to delivery drivers. Allocate time slots for customers and enforce the waiting provisions and limit their time slots within the building.

Where Social Distancing Is Not Possible

There will be times at which enforcing a strict two metre distancing rule is simply not possible. If you are in such a position, as well as identifying this explicitly in the COVID risk assessment, you must implement mitigating measures to keep everyone as safe as can sensibly be achieved.

By way of examples, employers should consider these additional control measures where two metre social distancing is not possible:

- Can the activity be stopped or paused during the pandemic?
- Can the amount of time during which that activity goes on be reduced?
- What is the minimum number of people who need to be present?
- Can those workers be kept away from other colleagues, including exiting/entering via different routes?
- What steps would limit the amount of items of equipment or surfaces that people need to touch?
- Could you use screens between people to create a physical barrier?
- Avoid face-to-face working.
- Mark the floor to create one-way systems or exclusion areas.

Emergencies, Security and Other Incidents

Review all incident, first aid and emergency procedures to ensure social distancing is respected as far as possible. Consider the security implications of any changes you intend to make to your operations and practices in response to the coronavirus pandemic as any revisions may present new or altered security risks. For organisations who carry out physical searches of people, consider how to ensure the safety of those conducting searches while maintaining security standards.

In particular consider whether designated gathering points for evacuation events offer sufficient space and how emergency services can enter and move around the building safely.

CHAPTER FOUR

COVID AND VEHICLE USAGE

Social Distancing when Using vehicles

Any individual or organisation responsible for planning work-related travel should make a decision as to whether travel in vehicles is needed for the business to continue to operate. If it is, then specific further thought will be needed as to whether particular journeys are essential and which individuals need to travel on such journeys.

Clearly the planning should be geared toward avoiding multi-occupancy vehicles where safe to do so. Where multi-occupancy vehicles are used, people should social distance where possible through suitable seating arrangements and where necessary, use of additional transport. Working patterns should be tailored so that only trips which require multiple passengers are undertaken by vehicles with multiple occupancy. Journeys should be kept as short as they can, vehicle windows opened to allow ventilation and employees work in specified "teams" rather than changing their working partners regularly.

If a vehicle will regularly be used by more than one person, who will be for example sitting in the cab area of a larger vehicle, consideration should be given to the installation of plastc screens between occupants.

Cleaning vehicles

Ensure vehicles are cleaned regularly, particularly between different users. Consider which parts should be cleaned daily or weekly. A written guide, either given to drivers, or else signed by them and evidenced as training would eb a wise addition to working practices. Somebody, whether drivers or maintenance staff must routinely be involved in cleaning those parts of the vehicle which are commonly handled or touched, such as handles, steering wheel, console buttons, centre touchscreen and stereo, handbrake and gearstick, keys and key fob, indicators and wiper stalks as well as windows, mirrors and mirror switches, seat adjusters and any other controls.

Drivers must be reminded to practice good hygiene before and after using the vehicle. Provision of hand sanitiser is vital.

Deliveries

Those driving for the purpose of delivering goods should give consideration to revising pick-up and drop-off collection points and procedures, so as to minimise contact with others. Likewise, when leaving a yard or depot, steps should be in pace to removing unnecessary contact at gatehouse security. In an ideal world, there will be increased uptake of non-contact delivery procedures where the nature of the product allows for use of electronic pre-booking.

More generally, all deliveries should, where possible and safe, have single workers to drive, load or unload vehicles. Where pairing-up is needed, using the same pairs of people on a settled basis will obviously result in reduced risk of transmission.

Whilst all of these practices are designed to prevent COVID spreading through workforces, it remains imperative that drivers can access welfare facilities when required, consistent with existing minimum standards, which have not been relaxed. Businesses which make or receive deliveries should ensure drivers have easy and safe access to toilets and handwashing facilities. The employer of the driver should make enquiries of recipient sites to ensure that facilities are provided, or are located close at hand. Drivers should also be encouraged to report where this is not the case to their own employer.

The legal responsibility to provide access to these facilities lies with whoever controls the premises drivers are visiting. HSE has received reports, also repeated across social media, that some drivers are not being allowed to use welfare facilities when they deliver. This is against the law and, with the latest advice for hands to be washed regularly, failure to allow access to welfare facilities may increase the risk of COVID-19 spreading.

The HSE has taken those various these reports seriously and accordingly issued a joint open letter along with Department for Transport, setting out the requirements[12].

Social Distancing In Drivers' Waiting Or Rest Rooms

You should manage the safety of visiting drivers in line with pre-existing HSE guidance by providing dedicated waiting areas with welfare and rest room facilities for them.

During the coronavirus pandemic employers must take steps to ensure drivers can follow good handwashing procedures and maintain social distancing. Make sure drivers understand what they should do to follow your site social distancing rules.

If existing facilities allow drivers to maintain social distancing, there may be no need to make any changes.

[12]https://assets.publishing.service.gov.uk/government/uploads/system/uploads/attachment_data/file/887867/dft-hse-letter-drivers-facilities.pdf#

Ventilation in Vehicles

Switch ventilation systems on while people are in the vehicle and set to drawing fresh air in, and not recirculating air.

To improve ventilation, windows can also be opened (partially if it's cold). Heating should also be left on to keep the vehicle warm. For vehicles that carry different passengers, such as taxis, clear the air between different passengers so the vehicle is aired before anyone else gets in.

Opening doors where it is safe to do so will help to change air quickly. Opening windows fully for a few minutes can also help to clear the air in the vehicle.

Changing where drivers wait

If an employer's existing facilities do not allow drivers to maintain social distancing, they could relocate the waiting area, or it may be safer – as a temporary measure – for drivers to remain in their cab during loading or unloading.

If you make changes to your current arrangements, think about how you'll continue to reduce the risk of drive-away incidents and how drivers can be allowed to safely access welfare facilities.

Relaxation of Drivers' Hours Rules

Requests for urgent exemptions should be made in line with the Department for Transport guidance.

Driver safety must not be compromised, and they should not be expected to drive while tired. Employers remain responsible for the health and safety of their employees, other road users, and anyone involved in loading and unloading vehicles.

CHAPTER FIVE

WORK PREMISES – PARTICULAR CORONAVIRUS CONSIDERATIONS

Key elements of an employer's duty to employees include the provision of a safe working environment with adequate facilities and arrangements for the welfare of staff, as well as the maintenance of it in a condition that safeguards the welfare of those working there[13].

Ventilation and Air Conditioning Systems

The legal obligation[14] on employers to ensure an adequate supply of fresh air in the workplace has not changed during the pandemic. Good quality ventilation, coupled with the imposition of social distancing measures, will play key roles in keeping a workplace clean and preventing transmission. The HSE Guidance makes clear that ventilation is considered as being every bit as important as handwashing or facial coverings in reducing the spread of infection.

This is because ventilation reduces the concentration of virus particles in the air and therefore manages the chances of airborne transmission. This is when people breathe in small particles (aerosols) from the air when someone infected with the virus has been in the same enclosed space. It is of note that ventilation will have little or no impact on

---

[13] Health and Safety at Work etc Act 1974, s2(2)(d) and (e).

[14] From the Workplace (Health, Safety and Welfare) Regulations 1992, Reg 6(1).

droplet or contact transmission routes, which is why it must be coupled with other measures.

A frequent misconception has been that providing adequate ventilation means that work premises have to be cold. Good ventilation is in reality a balancing act between making sure an indoor space is kept warm whilst simultaneously keeping a steady flow of air moving over the area. Natural ventilation, a rather grand title which encompasses such simple measures as partially opening a window, can be used in conjunction with heating systems to maintain a steady and comfortable temperature in the workplace.

Natural ventilation can be provided through open windows, or through other means such as vents. However, fire doors should never be propped open. Also consider security and physical safety along with the ventilation aspects.

It is now important that where possible staff should not completely close windows and doors when the area is occupied as this can result in very low levels of ventilation.

The relevant statutory duty is to ensure that every enclosed workplace is ventilated by a "sufficient quantity of fresh purified air[15].

Where any workplace (or part(s) of one) are poorly ventilated, it will be incumbent upon the employer to take steps beyond what would previously have been required to improve ventilation in those areas in order to achieve the new objective of a reduction in the risk of airborne transmission. There are some simple ways to identify poorly ventilated areas:

---

[15] Regulation 6 read in conjunction with *Pratt v Intermet Refractories* Lexis 21/1/2000.

- Any areas which have no mechanical or natural ventilation should be fairly obvious.

- Existing mechanical systems might provide the introduction of outdoor air, artificial temperature control or both. Systems that provide both heating and air conditioning are known as heating and ventilation air conditioning (HVAC). If a system is recirculating only and doesn't have an outdoor air supply, or a separate source of outdoor air, the area is likely to be poorly ventilated, unless a separate source of natural air is close by[16].

- Areas where the air appears stale or smells bad are prime candidates.

- Use of carbon dioxide monitors can identify the CO2 levels to indicate where ventilation is poor. Such monitors are at their most effective in areas which are regularly attended by the same group of people, or the same number of people in similarly-sized groups.

Where a workplace has a complex ventilation system, there is more guidance from the Chartered Institution of Building Services Engineers (CIBSE), which should be consulted and it may be advisable to engage a consultant to advise further.

16 See the Approved Code of Practice issued by the HSE at para 29.

Improvements to Ventilation

Airing rooms as frequently as you can will help improve ventilation. This involves opening all doors and windows wide to maximise the ventilation in the room. It may be easier to do this when the room is unoccupied or between uses.

If the area is still cold you could relax dress codes so people can wear extra layers and warmer clothing.

Fan convector heaters can be used provided the area is well ventilated, but they should not be used in poorly ventilated areas.

The use of fans, whether desk or ceiling fans can be used provided the area is well ventilated but they should not be used in poorly ventilated areas. In such areas it may be advisable to install local air cleaning and filtration units, which can be used to reduce airborne transmission where it isn't possible to maintain adequate ventilation. Filtration systems, high-efficiency filters and ultraviolet-based devices are the most suitable types to use.

Legionella Risks

Anyone in control of premises, including most construction sites, have a duty to protect people by identifying and controlling risks associated with legionella. Legionella is a water-borne bacteria which causes a number of diseases, including the most well-known and serious Legionnaires' Disease, but also a number of less serious conditions. Legionnaires' Disease is a potentially fatal form of pneumonia and everyone is susceptible to infection. The risk increases with age but some people are at higher risk, and these groups tend to coincide with the groups which appear to be at most risk from coronavirus.

If a building has been closed during the pandemic due to the lockdown restrictions, or the working from home directive, then water system stagnation can occur due to lack of use, increasing the risks of legionella growth.

Other sources of risk are the cleaning or reinstatement of a water system which has been out of service with water inside it, or the restarting of some types of air conditioning units. If the water system has still been used regularly, those responsible for managing the system should review whether the pandemic conditions have caused any interruption in the usual appropriate measures employed to prevent legionella growth. If hot and cold water outlets have been used infrequently, flushing them should prevent water stagnation.

As far as air conditioning units are concerned, where a workplace has been closed for an extended period and has air conditioning units that have a source of water that can generate aerosol, the responsible person will need to assess the risks of legionella being present within them before restarting.

Small wall or ceiling-mounted units with simple closed cooling systems are unlikely to cause any real risk. Larger units may present a risk if they have improperly drained condensate trays, or humidifier or evaporative cooling sections where water can stagnate, becoming a reservoir for bacteria to grow.

Employers with any sort of water systems should review this risk in their updated Covid-compliant risk assessment and manage the legionella risks by planning a cleaning regime and how or when restart should occur.

Specific guidance has been issued by the HSE in respect of cooling towers and evaporative condensers. Operators of such substantial water-based cooling systems should have designed particular policies around lockdown and to manage them in any periods of reduced staffing. HSE Inspectors, should they inspect premises, would likely expect to see these documents.

Restarting Workplace Equipment

The HSE have suggested that all users of pressure systems in the workplace regard the start-up of all such systems following a period of inactivity as a functional pressure test and that the safety precautions detailed in a full Guidance Note[17] published for that purpose be followed.

This is because starting up any pressure system from cold can significantly affect the mechanical behaviour of vessels, pipework and moving parts. Hydraulic fluid may also be less predictable when cold. The physical risk from moving parts and valves which behave in unexpected ways must be anticipated in a proper assessment.

[17] At https://www.hse.gov.uk/pubns/gs4.htm

CHAPTER SIX

PROTECTING HOME WORKERS

An employer has the same health and safety responsibilities for home workers as for any other workers. When someone is working from home, permanently or temporarily, an employer should consider:

- How will you keep in touch with them?
- What work activity will they be doing (and for how long)?
- Can it be done safely in their home environment?
- Do you need to use control measures in place to protect them?

Lone working

There will always be greater risks for lone workers with no direct supervision or anyone to help them if things go wrong. Steps must be taken to keep open lines of communication between employers and their staff, including those working from home, in part to make sure they are healthy and safe.

If contact is poor, workers may feel disconnected, isolated or abandoned. This can affect mental health, stress and emotional wellbeing. Under the Management of Health and Safety at Work Regulations 1999, employers must manage the risk to lone workers, considering who will be involved and which hazards could harm those working alone.

Within the coronavirus pandemic context, particular factors must be borne in mind. Risks that particularly affect lone workers include exacerbation of mental health issues, a person's competence to work alone with support and supervision and the nature of where they live. A person in a rural area may struggle to access best quality broadband. An urban dweller may live in a shared home of multiple occupancy and therefore lack suitable space to work consistently. Questionnaires and dialogue are key to understanding and managing the difficulties faced.

Lone working in the domestic setting has suddenly emerged on a mass scale as a result of the government's directive that staff work from home where they can. Many employers will have been taken somewhat by surprise by the sudden emphasis upon the importance of relationships with, and support from, other workers. The combination of sudden home working in a time of unprecedented national restrictions will have generated particular stresses for staff in all sectors.

Being away from managers and colleagues will make it difficult to get proper support. The need for pastoral care to deal with the stress of home working and the sudden loss of the traditional working structure will both cause particular difficulties and each employer will need to consider how these relationships can be fostered in very different circumstances.

The levels of supervision needed will be dictated by the contents of the relevant risk assessment. The higher the risk, the more supervision they will need. This will also depend on their ability to identify and handle health and safety issues.

Once such systems are in place, the onus is on those involved to communicate any difficulties to management. Plans should be in place to regularly test these communication systems and all emergency procedures to ensure lone workers can be contacted if a problem or emergency is identified and vice versa.

It is also a good idea for a new worker to be supervised at first if they're being trained, doing a job with specific risks or learning how to deal with new situations. This supervision can be facilitated through remote internet communications if appropriate.

This will include a need to put procedures in place that enable direct contact with a lone worker so their manager can recognise signs of stress as early as possible. If contact is poor, workers may feel disconnected, isolated or abandoned. This can affect their performance and potentially their stress levels and mental health.

If an employer has reason to be aware that someone's health condition means, or may mean, that they are not entirely safe to work alone, they should get medical advice. The assessment should consider both routine work and possible emergencies that may put additional physical and mental burdens on the lone worker.

First aid and emergencies

Put emergency procedures in place and train lone workers in how to use them. A company's risk assessment may indicate lone workers should:

- carry first aid equipment.
- receive first aid training, including how to use first aid on themselves, which might be delivered online.
- have access to adequate first aid facilities.

Emergency procedures should include guidance on how and when lone workers should contact their employer, including details of any emergency contact numbers, which must then be monitored appropriately.

Training

It is harder for lone workers to get help, so they may need extra training. They should understand any risks in their work and how to control them. Training is particularly important where there is limited supervision to control, guide and help in uncertain situations. Training can also be tailored to help staff understand how to respond to unexpected situations, such as those involving violence at a time with reduced staff numbers on site.

Employers should set limits on what can be done while working alone. These should help to ensure that staff are competent to deal with the requirements of the job, trained in using any new technical solutions and able to recognise when they should seek assistance from colleagues.

Working with Display Screen Equipment

For those people who are working at home on a long-term basis, the risks associated with using display screen equipment (DSE) must be controlled. This includes asking employees to undertake workstation assessments at home.

There is no increased risk from DSE work for those working at home temporarily. This means that in that situation employers do not need to ask them to carry out home workstation assessments. However, employers should provide workers with advice on completing their own basic assessment at home.

There are some simple steps people can take to reduce the risks from display screen work, such as breaking up long spells of DSE work with rest breaks, avoiding strain by regularly changing position and getting up to move around regularly[18]. Staff can avoid eye fatigue by changing focus or blinking from time to time.

Employers should try to meet those needs where possible. For some equipment (eg keyboards, mouse, riser) this could mean allowing workers to take this equipment home. For other larger items (eg ergonomic chairs, height-adjustable desks) encourage workers to try other ways of creating a comfortable working environment (eg supporting cushions).

As any period of temporary home working extends, employers should have regular discussions with workers to assess whether additional steps are needed, for example where they report:

- aches, pains or discomfort related to their temporary DSE arrangements
- adverse effects of working in isolation, on remote IT systems
- working longer hours without adequate rest and recovery breaks

Where employers decide to make working from home arrangements permanent, they should explain how to carry out full workstation

[18] The Court of Appeal in *Denton Hall v Fifield* [2006] EWCA Civ 169 expressly rejected the idea that a worker left to their own devices who works for too long has brought on their own injury.

assessments[19] and provide workers with appropriate equipment and advice on control measures.

[19] Likely to require expert ergonomic input to be satisfactory, per *Allison* [2008] EWCA Civ 71.

CHAPTER SEVEN

WORKERS WITH PRE-EXISTING VULNERABILITIES

Any employer has a legal duty to protect workers from harm. In light of the outbreak of a pandemic, employers should be sure to identify those workers who are particularly vulnerable to contract the virus or to suffer more badly than others due to some particular criteria or characteristic of which the employer is or should be aware. Once these people are identified the employer must then go further and consider whether to put controls in place to reduce that risk.

Supporting Workers in Higher-risk Groups

Public Health England has identified some groups of people may be at more risk of being infected and/or an adverse outcome if infected. The higher-risk groups include those who:

- are older males
- have a high body mass index (BMI)
- have health conditions such as diabetes
- are from some Black, Asian or minority ethnicity (BAME) backgrounds

Public Health England, supported by the HSE and the Faculty of Medicine, have worked together to consider strategies to lessen workplace risks of COVID-19 for BAME groups. There are currently no published Guidance documents which express any expectations of additional controls specifically applied to further protect these groups. However, it would be wise for duty-holders to ensure that existing controls (social distancing, good hygiene and cleaning, ventilation, supervision etc) are applied strictly and that groups including vulnerable staff members are regularly reminded of what measures are in place and the collective need to respect them.

As part of this approach, employers should ensure all workers, including those in higher-risk groups, are able to access all the protections that are necessary, including during night shifts, when working remotely or working alone. This might include access to personal protective equipment (PPE) stocks or cleaning materials.

Clinically Extremely Vulnerable Workers

During the pandemic, the government has defined some people as clinically extremely vulnerable. These people were previously described during the first lockdown as shielded or shielding, a term which appears no longer to have any particular meaning. Any workers within this definition are at increased risk of severe illness from coronavirus. From 5 January 2021 the government made it a recommendation that anyone who is clinically extremely vulnerable should not attend work and should only work from home, as coronavirus cases were rising rapidly across the country.

An employer should talk to clinically extremely vulnerable workers about their working arrangements and take every possible step to enable them to work from home. Consulting with workers will be expected as you undertake the decision about which work tasks they can do at home.

In making that decision an employer should consider tasks that could be done in another way that means you don't need to go into work, for example customer consultations online, checking in with sites virtually, talking to managers about work that needs to be done using email, phone and conferencing

- Agree on providing the IT and other equipment they will need to work remotely
- think about how you will keep in touch with people working remotely, to make sure they feel part of the team and involved
- think about using online resources to look after their mental health and wellbeing

Pregnant Workers

During the pandemic, pregnant workers have been advised to follow strict social distancing to reduce the risk of severe illness from coronavirus.

There is a long-standing requirement for employers to put in place measures to ensure workplace safety where a significant health and safety risk is identified for a new or expectant mother.

Some pregnant workers will be at greater risk of severe illness from coronavirus. They are defined as clinically extremely vulnerable and they should stay at home as much as possible and work from home if they can. Employers will need to take this into account in their risk assessment.

If any significant risks are identified, the duty-holder must take the appropriate action as soon as they are notified, in writing, that an employee is a new or expectant mother, to ensure that she is not further exposed.

If that organisation is unable to avoid or control any risks that go beyond the level of risk found outside the workplace, then it must take appropriate action. This might include altering working conditions and/or hours of work or finding suitable alternative work.

If an organisation cannot put the necessary control measures in place, such as adjustments to the job or working from home, they should suspend the pregnant worker on paid leave. This is in line with normal requirements under regulation 16(3) of the Management of Health and Safety at Work Regulations 1999.

New and Young Workers

Workers are at particular risk of injury in the first six months of a job, when they are more likely to be unaware of existing or potential risks[20]. Young people will often be in this category. In health and safety law, a young person is anyone under 18 and a child is anyone who has not yet reached the official minimum school leaving age.

As an employer, in addition to your health and safety responsibilities to all your employees, you are responsible for ensuring a young person

[20] As a result of this, younger workers are specifically provided for in Regs 3(4) and (5) of the Management of Health and Safety at Work Regulations 1999 and this attitude is likely to be mirrored in how employers are expected to deal with young employees affected by pandemic conditions.

is not exposed to risk due to lack of experience, being unaware of existing or potential risks or lack of maturity.

Migrant Workers

Those who employ migrant workers are obliged to focus on four main areas to ensure the health and safety of those workers, namely training, communication, competence and attitudes to health and safety. Due to the linguistic and cultural differences between workforces in other countries and in the UK, the principal concerns are that workers from other nations may not value health and safety, or have basic training in safe practice.

The relevance of this in the context of the coronavirus pandemic is straightforward. Given the volume of misinformation and propaganda circulated by various groups and individuals through new media, there is a risk that any person may be sceptical as to the nature of the virus and the need for particular measures. Within social groups comprised of those who don't communicate readily and are not necessarily quick to accept government messaging, there is a risk that even the best and most carefully-devised measures could be simply disregarded.

Therefore with migrant workers comes a particular obligation to com municate the importance of the measures imposed, monitor compliance and ensure that those who do disregard the measures are left in no doubt as to the consequences of sustained non-compliance.

People with disabilities

If you employ people with disabilities you have a duty under the Equality Act 2010 to make reasonable adjustments to your workplace for them. Every aspect of the changes made to a workplace to render it safe in the times of COVID must also be reviewed to ensure that they do not disadvantage any disabled staff members.

CHAPTER EIGHT

OTHER OFFENCES AND HEALTH AND SAFETY

The Coronavirus Act 2020

In order to bring into force the raft of new measures required to deal with the multitude of challenges posed by the pandemic, the government put together the Coronavirus Act 2020. Rarely has a piece of legislation made such significant changes in such a wide range of different areas. For the most part, it relaxed requirements, making it easier to transport food or register new healthcare workers among many other changes. However, buried deep in the detail, as is often the case, are a few key provisions which create new criminal offences.

Within Schedule 22 of the Act are particular provisions regarding events and gatherings. Chapter 5 of that schedule confers the Power to prohibit or otherwise restrict events or gatherings in England and so far as is relevant it provides that:

> *"(1) The Secretary of State may, for the purpose of—*
>
> *(a) preventing, protecting against, delaying or otherwise controlling the incidence or transmission of coronavirus, or*
>
> *(b) facilitating the most appropriate deployment of medical or emergency personnel and resources,*
>
> *issue a direction prohibiting, or imposing requirements or restrictions in relation to, the holding of an event or gathering in England.*

(2) A direction under sub-paragraph (1) may be issued in relation to—

(a) a specified event or gathering, or

(b) events or gatherings of a specified description.

(3) A direction under sub-paragraph (1) may only have the effect of imposing prohibitions, requirements or restrictions on—

(a) the owner or occupier of premises for an event or gathering to which the direction relates;

(b) the organiser of such an event or gathering;

(c) any other person involved in holding such an event or gathering.

(4) A direction under sub-paragraph (1) may only be issued during a public health response period.

(5) A direction under sub-paragraph (1) may, among other things, impose requirements about informing persons who may be planning to attend an event or gathering of its prohibition or any requirements or restrictions imposed in relation to the holding of it.

(6) For the purposes of sub-paragraph (2), events or gatherings may be described—

(a) by reference to a number of people attending the event or gathering,

(b) by reference to a requirement for medical or emergency services to attend the event or gathering, or

(c) in any other way.

(7) The reference in sub-paragraph (3)(c) to a person involved in the holding of an event or gathering does not include a person whose only involvement in the event or gathering is, or would be, by attendance at the event or gathering."

Those provision are directly followed by Paragraph 6 of Schedule 22, which is concerned with the power to close premises in England or impose restrictions on persons entering or remaining in them

"(1) The Secretary of State may, for the purpose of—

(a) preventing, protecting against, delaying or otherwise controlling the incidence or transmission of coronavirus, or

(b) facilitating the most appropriate deployment of medical or emergency personnel and resources,

issue a direction imposing prohibitions, requirements or restrictions in relation to the entry into, departure from, or location of persons in, premises in England.

(2) A direction under sub-paragraph (1) may be issued in relation to—

(a) specified premises, or

(b) premises of a specified description.

(3) A direction under sub-paragraph (1) may only have the effect of imposing prohibitions, requirements or restrictions on—

(a) the owner or occupier of premises to which the direction relates;

(b) any other person involved in managing entry into, or departure from, such premises or the location of persons in them.

(4) A direction under sub-paragraph (1) may only be issued during a public health response period.

(5) A direction under sub-paragraph (1) may, among other things, impose requirements for the purpose of—

(a) closing the premises;

(b) restricting entry into the premises;

(c) securing restrictions in relation to the location of persons in the premises.

(6) A direction under sub-paragraph (1) may impose prohibitions, requirements or restrictions by reference to (among other things)—

(a) the number of persons in the premises;

(b) the size of the premises;

(c) the purpose for which a person is in the premises;

(d) the facilities in the premises;

(e) a period of time."

The provisions of the preceding paragraphs are given the full effect of the criminal law by virtue of Paragraph 9 of Schedule 22, which states that "[a] person commits an offence if the person fails without reasonable excuse to comply with a prohibition, requirement or restriction imposed on the person by a direction issued under this Part of this Schedule.

An offence contrary to Schedule 22 can be prosecuted as a summary-only offence and attracts a maximum penalty of an unlimited fine.

Should the offence be committed by a body corporate, either by virtue of the consent, connivance or negligence of an employee of that body, then both the entity and the individual may be prosecuted and punished on a joint and several basis. An officer, for those purposes, means a director, manager, secretary or "other similar officer", so a degree of responsibility and control is certainly required.

These provisions will very likely continue to be used as virus control measures are eased and any event or premises which fails to properly plan to operate in a way which is Covid-secure, or which fails to respect Guidelines issued by the HSE or other relevant bodies when planning particular events may well find themselves on the wrong side of statutory directions or even prosecution. The concept of "vaccine passports" or similar measures may also be brought in and a failure to respect and incorporate any such guidance will likely lead to the invocation of these measures in the period following the lifting of stricter lockdown measures.

Corporate Manslaughter

Corporate Manslaughter is an offence created by Section 1 of the Corporate Manslaughter and Corporate Homicide Act 2007. It came into force on 6th April 2008. This offence was drafted so as to make sure that companies and other organisations are criminally accountable for very serious failings resulting in death.

In a prosecution for corporate manslaughter, the following needs to be proved:

1. the defendant is a qualifying organisation;
2. the organisation owed a relevant duty of care to the deceased;

3. there was a gross breach of that duty by the organisation;

4. the way in which its activities were managed or organised by its senior management was a substantial element in the breach; and

5. the gross breach of the organisation's duty caused or contributed to the death.

At the start of the first peak of the coronavirus outbreak in the UK, the Royal College of Nursing issued guidance for its members, in response to chronic shortages of PPE. This guidance suggested that, if all else failed, nursing staff could justify walking out and refusing to treat patients if their employers did not provide adequate equipment.

However, the guidance did suggest that any members moved to take this step should record their reasons in writing, in case they were subsequently prosecuted for corporate manslaughter. The RCN did warn that such liability might arise in "rare cases". As a matter of legal precision, an individual nurse could not be prosecuted for that offence, and proving any homicide offence caused by a single medical professional refusing to work would be frankly impossible. However the potential liabilities for hospitals, government departments and even the RCN itself might have been more realistic had that led to a widespread walkout.

CHAPTER NINE

COVID-19 AND THE RIDDOR REPORTING REGIME

The obligation to notify the Health and Safety Executive of injuries and incidents in the workplace is derived from the Reporting of Injuries, Diseases and Dangerous Occurrences Regulations 2013 ("RIDDOR").

RIDDOR puts duties on employers, the self-employed and people in control of work premises ('the Responsible Person') to report (i) certain serious workplace accidents, (ii) occupational diseases and (iii) specified dangerous occurrences (near misses).

When a reportable incident takes place, the Responsible Person must report this to HSE via telephone, or more usually through an online form. The report should be made without delay and, in any event, within 10 days (save in cases whereby the incident is only reportable due to it causing seven or more days of incapacitation, when the report must be made within 15 days).

Failure to do report is an offence contrary to HSWA 1974 s. 33(1)(c) and carries a maximum sentence of two years in custody or an unlimited fine.

There is a defence under Regulation 11 of RIDDOR "for that person to prove that he was not aware of the event requiring him to notify or send a report to the relevant enforcing authority, and that he had taken all reasonable steps to have all such events brought to his notice". The burden placed on a defendant seeking to avail themselves of this defence is to show on the balance of probabilities that they were unaware of the event. It is for them to show that they took all reasonable steps.

Serious workplace accidents

If someone has died or has been injured because of a work-related accident this may have to be reported. Not all accidents need to be reported, however. A RIDDOR report is only required when:

(i) there has been an accident (which caused the injury);

(ii) the accident was work-related; and

(iii) the injury is of a type which is reportable.

Point (i) above requires that there must be an accident. An accident is a separate, identifiable, unintended incident, which causes physical injury. This specifically includes acts of non-consensual violence to people at work. Injuries themselves, eg 'feeling a sharp twinge', are not accidents. There must be an identifiable external event that causes the injury, e.g. a falling object striking someone.

Cumulative exposures to hazards, which eventually cause injury (eg repetitive lifting), are not classed as 'accidents' under RIDDOR, although this should have little relevance in cases related to COVID-19.

Point (ii) restricts the requirement to report to accidents which are 'work-related'. A Responsible Person should report accidents if they happen 'out of or in connection with work'. The fact that there is an accident at work premises does not, in itself, mean that the accident is work-related – the work activity itself must contribute to the accident. An accident is 'work-related' if it arises from the way the work was carried out; or any machinery, plant, substances or equipment used for the work; orthe condition of the site or premises where the accident happened.

Finally, an accident will only be reportable if the work-related accident causes a 'reportable' injury. This includes the death of any person, specified injuries to workers (fractures, amputations, serious burns, crush injuries affecting internal organs and so on, see Regulation 4 of RIDDOR), injuries to workers which result in their incapacitation for more than 7 days or Injuries to non-workers which result in them being taken directly to hospital for treatment.

Occupational Diseases

Employers and self-employed people must report diagnoses of certain occupational diseases, where these are likely to have been caused or made worse by their work. These include (according to Regulations 8 and 9 of RIDDOR) a list of conditions which might readily be thought of as occupational diseases, such as carpal tunnel syndrome, hand-arm vibration syndrome or occupational asthma. However the definition also includes, according to Regulation 9(b), "any disease attributed to an occupational exposure to a biological agent."

Dangerous Occurrences

Dangerous occurrences are certain, specified near-miss events. Not all such events require reporting. There are 27 categories of dangerous occurrences that are relevant to most workplaces, one of which (Para 10 of Schedule 3A to RIDDOR) is any accident or incident which results or could have resulted in the release or escape of a biological agent likely to cause severe human infection or illness.

Particular Workplaces Vulnerable to COVID

Care providers and hospitals are put in an unenviable position by their RIDDOR obligations. They are understandably concerned that notifying the HSE of a incident which did not in fact qualify under RIDDOR could result in an unnecessary HSE investigation. Some care providers are also concerned that a notification under RIDDOR may be misinterpreted as an admission of responsibility should criminal and/or civil action be pursued.

Care must be taken to advise these organisations of the risk of prosecution for failing to report and the limited nature of the perils of an investigation following an isolated incident which is properly reported.

CHAPTER TEN

INSPECTION AND ENFORCEMENT

HSE Inspections and COVID-19

The HSE has not used the onset of the pandemic as an excuse to scale down its operations. Quite the opposite, it seems that new inspectors are being recruited and relationships with secondary agencies are being utilised to increase the Executive's activities and allow them to monitor how duty-holders are managing the novel risks which have been created by the prevailing circumstances.

The HSE has been at pains to publicise, through their website, print advertisements and especially social media that it is continuing to carry out spot checks and inspections on all types of businesses across the UK to ensure they are COVID secure. This has included both industry-specific campaigns and also geographically-focused activities.

As well as physical visits, the Executive has begun to undertake telephone spot checks on businesses. During these calls they will offer expert advice on how to manage the risks and protect workers, customers and visitors. However the online guidance also states that "[b]y calling and visiting premises and speaking directly to employers, we can check the measures they've put in place are in line with government guidance."

This makes it clear that the dual purpose of these telephone contacts is first to offer assistance, but at the same time to undertake something of a 'triage' to identify and flag those organisations which have failed to understand and act upon the new duties arising from the measures put in place to control the virus.

HSE Inspectors will incorporate checks designed to interrogate the measures a visited party has in place to control the transmission of COVID-19 into their daily regime of visiting workplaces during the pandemic.

Any organisation who should be the recipient of either a telephone call or a spot visit from an Inspector, should participate in the spot check and engage with the process. A failure to do so could lead to enforcement action and may constitute an offence in its own right.

When an Inspector calls (in any sense) there should always be a person present on each set of premises who either has the necessary information to hand, or knows who to contact to obtain it. The quickest way to demonstrate compliance is to be able to produce a risk assessment which specifically deals with issues around COVID-19.

During any inspection, measures to enforce and ensure social distancing should largely be obvious to any visitor, but if any weaknesses are identified then a constructive attitude will generally meet with more success than an obstructive approach.

Additionally, the Inspector will expect to see handwashing and hygiene procedures, both on paper and in action.

During an inspection, it is usual for the Inspector to wish to speak to the management, staff and any staff representative bodies. Where businesses are not managing the risks of spreading coronavirus, the HSE will take immediate action by offering advice, stopping certain work practices until they are made safe, issuing enforcement notices and prosecuting where a busines fails to comply.

To ensure they are able to carry out inspections in as many workplaces as possible across the UK the HSE is renewing associations and utilising existing partnerships with external organisations, especially Local Authorities.

The work with Councils and other local government bodies allows the HSE to utilise the skills of staff employed by those bodies to assist with monitoring businesses operating in those sectors that they usually regulate such as hospitality (hotels, shops, pubs, restaurants and takeaways) and retail.

Public relations material posted on the HSE website and social media has emphasised the ability of the HSE to co-ordinate inspection work in particular sectors and geographic areas. Transport companies have been a particular focus and an HSE post circulated through social media platforms in January 2021 noted that it was the intention of the HSE to undertake spot inspections in Scotland, Northern England and the Midlands to check businesses that transport goods are COVID-secure.

Enforcement Options

The stated aim of the HSE is to ensure that duty-holders manage and control risks effectively and so prevent harm. The intended purpose of enforcement action is to:

1. Ensure that duty-holders take action to deal immediately with serious risks;
2. Promote and achieve sustained compliance with the law;
3. Ensure that those who breach health and safety requirements, including directors and managers are held to account

The HSE's attitude to enforcement action is set out in its publication "HSE Enforcement Policy Statement"[21]. This document, last updated in October 2015, has been cited in a number of bulletins issued during the lifetime of the COVID-19 restrictions, and there is no suggestion t has been modified or superseded in any way.

The policy statement says that the public interest would normally require enforcing authorities to prosecute where one or more of the following circumstances apply:

1. Death resulted from the breach of legislation.
2. The offence created is a grave one and gave rise to serious actual or potential harm.
3. The general record and approach of the offender warrants it.
4. The duty-holder's standard of managing health and safety issues found to be far below what is required by law and gave rise to serious risk
5. Reckless disregard of health and safety requirements has taken place.
6. Repeated breaches, which give rise to significant risk, have occurred.
7. There has been persistent and significant poor compliance.
8. Work has been carried out without or in serious non-compliance with an appropriate licence or safety case.

[21] <http://www.hse.gov.uk/enforce/enforcepolicy.htm>

9. There has been a failure to comply with an improvement notice or prohibition notice.

10. There has been a repetition of a breach that was the subject of a formal caution

Where the HSE have undertaken an inspection and identified concerns, they will often invite representations from the organisation involved, or their legal representatives. Such representations should, to maximise their effect, make reference to this policy to place the perceived breaches or failings as low in the spectrum of concerns as can sensibly be suggested.

Methods of Enforcement

The methods of enforcement available to the HSE are:

1. Early intervention, as in the construction industry where the HSE has sought to influence duty holders in the design of projects before the construction process begins;

2. Verbal warnings;

3. Letters of Advice/recommendations;

4. Improvement and prohibition notices[22];

5. Formal Cautions;

6. Permissioning and licencing regimes. Where a particular work activity involves significant hazards a permissioning regime

[22] As provided for by the Health and Safety at Work Act 1974 ss 21 and 24.

may be imposed. Such activities cannot take place unless a consent, licence, letter or conclusion, or acceptance of a safety case or safety report has been given or accepted. These areas include the nuclear industry, railways, offshore installations and those working with asbestos; and

7. Crown Censure. A feature of the HSWA 1974 is that Crown bodies are subject to requirements of health and safety law including the general duties under ss 2-7, but may not be prosecuted or made the subject of other enforcement action. Crown bodies may, however be made the subject of crown censure. This is an administrative procedure whereby the HSE sets out a written account of the breaches alleged and the evidence set out in support of them. The appropriate crown body may accept the censure or not.

Particular Considerations Post-Pandemic

There are a few particular issues regarding the likely way in which the HSE and other bodies with similar responsibilities will approach the enforcement of failures to implement COVID-19 guidance on their premises.

First, proving that any breaches caused any particular infections will always be a difficulty, given the high transmission rates in the general population. Unless dealing with a particular strain or variant, the very factor which renders the need for protection so urgent, that s to say the virulent nature of the infection, will also make it far harder to pinpoint the precise consequences of any dangerous practices.

Second, the criminal courts, to which the most-grave matters are referred for prosecution, are creaking under the strain of successive funding cuts and the pandemic itself. Trials and in-person hearings generally have been restricted to some degree since March 2020.

The Crown Prosecution Service, for example, has issued Interim Case Review Guidance[23] in which it encourages its own prosecutors to consider the expanding pipeline of cases waiting to be heard and the consequent delays within the criminal justice system. It explicitly anticipates that a proportion of cases which would have been prosecuted before March 2020 might now be compromised on lesser charges or else dropped altogether. The rationale behind this is equally applicable to other prosecuting bodies, such as the HSE.

Finally the imposition of penalties against corporate bodies was drastically shaken up by the publication of the Sentencing Council's Definitive Guideline on Health and Safety Offences, which has led to a dramatic increase in the size of fines imposed in such cases by the criminal courts. However, in considering the appropriate size of fine the Court is bound to take account of the financial position of the defendant will now include the impact of the pandemic on the recent health of the finances and its likely future impact.

A return to the pre-Guideline approach, and the principles *in R v F Howe and Sons (Engineers) Ltd*[24] seems inevitable.

---

[23] https://www.cps.gov.uk/legal-guidance/coronavirus-interim-cps-case-review-guidance-application-public-interest-covid-19

[24] [1999] 2 Cr App R (S) 37

'Covid-19, Homeworking and the Law – The Essential Guide to Employment and GDPR Issues' by Forbes Solicitors
'Covid-19, Force Majeure and Frustration of Contracts – The Essential Guide' by Keith Markham
'Covid-19 and Criminal Law – The Essential Guide' by Ramya Nagesh
'Covid-19 and Family Law in England and Wales – The Essential Guide' by Safda Mahmood
'A Practical Guide to the Law of Unlawful Eviction and Harassment – 2nd Edition' by Stephanie Lovegrove
'Covid-19, Residential Property, Equity Release and Enfranchisement – The Essential Guide' by Paul Sams and Louise Uphill
'Covid-19, Brexit and the Law of Commercial Leases – The Essential Guide' by Mark Shelton
'A Practical Guide to Costs in Personal Injury Claims – 2nd Edition' by Matthew Hoe
'A Practical Guide to the General Data Protection Regulation (GDPR) – 2nd Edition' by Keith Markham
'Ellis on Credit Hire – Sixth Edition' by Aidan Ellis & Tim Kevan
'A Practical Guide to Working with Litigants in Person and McKenzie Friends in Family Cases' by Stuart Barlow
'Protecting Unregistered Brands: A Practical Guide to the Law of Passing Off' by Lorna Brazell
'A Practical Guide to Secondary Liability and Joint Enterprise Post-Jogee' by Joanne Cecil & James Mehigan
'A Practical Guide to the Pre-Action RTA Claims Protocol for Personal Injury Lawyers' by Antonia Ford
'A Practical Guide to Neighbour Disputes and the Law' by Alexander Walsh
'A Practical Guide to Forfeiture of Leases' by Mark Shelton
'A Practical Guide to Coercive Control for Legal Practitioners and Victims' by Rachel Horman

'A Practical Guide to Rights Over Airspace and Subsoil' by Daniel Gatty
'Tackling Disclosure in the Criminal Courts – A Practitioner's Guide' by Narita Bahra QC & Don Ramble
'A Practical Guide to the Law of Driverless Cars – Second Edition' by Alex Glassbrook, Emma Northey & Scarlett Milligan
'A Practical Guide to TOLATA Claims' by Greg Williams
'Artificial Intelligence – The Practical Legal Issues' by John Buyers
'A Practical Guide to the Law of Prescription in Scotland' by Andrew Foyle
'A Practical Guide to the Construction and Rectification of Wills and Trust Instruments' by Edward Hewitt
'A Practical Guide to the Law of Bullying and Harassment in the Workplace' by Philip Hyland
'How to Be a Freelance Solicitor: A Practical Guide to the SRA-Regulated Freelance Solicitor Model' by Paul Bennett
'A Practical Guide to Prison Injury Claims' by Malcolm Johnson
'A Practical Guide to the Small Claims Track' by Dominic Bright
'A Practical Guide to Advising Clients at the Police Station' by Colin Stephen McKeown-Beaumont
'A Practical Guide to Antisocial Behaviour Injunctions' by Iain Wightwick
'Practical Mediation: A Guide for Mediators, Advocates, Advisers, Lawyers, and Students in Civil, Commercial, Business, Property, Workplace, and Employment Cases' by Jonathan Dingle with John Sephton
'The Mini-Pupillage Workbook' by David Boyle
'A Practical Guide to Crofting Law' by Brian Inkster
'A Practical Guide to Spousal Maintenance' by Liz Cowell
'A Practical Guide to the Law of Domain Names and Cybersquatting' by Andrew Clemson
'A Practical Guide to the Law of Gender Pay Gap Reporting' by Harini Iyengar

'A Practical Guide to the Rights of Grandparents in Children Proceedings' by Stuart Barlow
'NHS Whistleblowing and the Law' by Joseph England
'Employment Law and the Gig Economy' by Nigel Mackay & Annie Powell
'A Practical Guide to Noise Induced Hearing Loss (NIHL) Claims' by Andrew Mckie, Ian Skeate, Gareth McAloon
'An Introduction to Beauty Negligence Claims – A Practical Guide for the Personal Injury Practitioner' by Greg Almond
'Intercompany Agreements for Transfer Pricing Compliance' by Paul Sutton
'Zen and the Art of Mediation' by Martin Plowman
'A Practical Guide to the SRA Principles, Individual and Law Firm Codes of Conduct 2019 – What Every Law Firm Needs to Know' by Paul Bennett
'A Practical Guide to Adoption for Family Lawyers' by Graham Pegg
'A Practical Guide to Industrial Disease Claims' by Andrew Mckie & Ian Skeate
'A Practical Guide to Redundancy' by Philip Hyland
'A Practical Guide to Vicarious Liability' by Mariel Irvine
'A Practical Guide to Applications for Landlord's Consent and Variation of Leases' by Mark Shelton
'A Practical Guide to Relief from Sanctions Post-Mitchell and Denton' by Peter Causton
'A Practical Guide to Equity Release for Advisors' by Paul Sams
'A Practical Guide to the Law Relating to Food' by Ian Thomas
'A Practical Guide to Financial Services Claims' by Chris Hegarty
'The Law of Houses in Multiple Occupation: A Practical Guide to HMO Proceedings' by Julian Hunt
'A Practical Guide to Unlawful Eviction and Harassment' by Stephanie Lovegrove
'Occupiers, Highways and Defective Premises Claims: A Practical Guide Post-Jackson – 2nd Edition' by Andrew Mckie

'A Practical Guide to Financial Ombudsman Service Claims' by Adam Temple & Robert Scrivenor
'A Practical Guide to Advising Schools on Employment Law' by Jonathan Holden
'A Practical Guide to Running Housing Disrepair and Cavity Wall Claims: 2nd Edition' by Andrew Mckie & Ian Skeate
'A Practical Guide to Holiday Sickness Claims – 2nd Edition' by Andrew Mckie & Ian Skeate
'Arguments and Tactics for Personal Injury and Clinical Negligence Claims' by Dorian Williams
'A Practical Guide to Drone Law' by Rufus Ballaster, Andrew Firman, Eleanor Clot
'A Practical Guide to Compliance for Personal Injury Firms Working With Claims Management Companies' by Paul Bennett
'A Practical Guide to Dog Law for Owners and Others' by Andrea Pitt
'RTA Allegations of Fraud in a Post-Jackson Era: The Handbook – 2nd Edition' by Andrew Mckie
'RTA Personal Injury Claims: A Practical Guide Post-Jackson' by Andrew Mckie
'On Experts: CPR35 for Lawyers and Experts' by David Boyle
'An Introduction to Personal Injury Law' by David Boyle
'A Practical Guide to Subtle Brain Injury Claims' by Pankaj Madan

These books and more are available to order online direct from the publisher at www.lawbriefpublishing.com, where you can also read free sample chapters. For any queries, contact us on 0844 587 2383 or mail@lawbriefpublishing.com.

Our books are also usually in stock at www.amazon.co.uk with free next day delivery for Prime members, and at good legal bookshops such as Wildy & Sons.

We are regularly launching new books in our series of practical day-to-day practitioners' guides. Visit our website and join our free newsletter to be kept informed and to receive special offers, free chapters, etc.

You can also follow us on Twitter at www.twitter.com/lawbriefpub.

www.ingramcontent.com/pod-product-compliance
Ingram Content Group UK Ltd.
Pitfield, Milton Keynes, MK11 3LW, UK
UKHW020151290926
15471UKWH00004B/810

9 781913 715908